Fire

by Luana K. Mitten and Mary Wagner

Table of Contents

ROURKE CLASSROOM RESOURCES
The path to student success

Lighting Fires

Fires can start in many different ways.
People light fires using matches.

Lightning bolts or **erupting** volcanoes can start fires.

Forest Rangers start fires to clear
a space. The burned space stops
a spreading fire.

Using Fire

We use fire in many ways. Campers use fires for heat, light and cooking.

We use fires in celebrations. We celebrate the Fourth of July with fireworks and sparklers.

We celebrate some holidays by lighting candles.

We use fire to create things.

Energy and Heat

Heat from fire is a form of **energy**.

Heat energy makes the train go.

Heat energy helps launch a rocket into space.

We use the heat from fires to cook food.

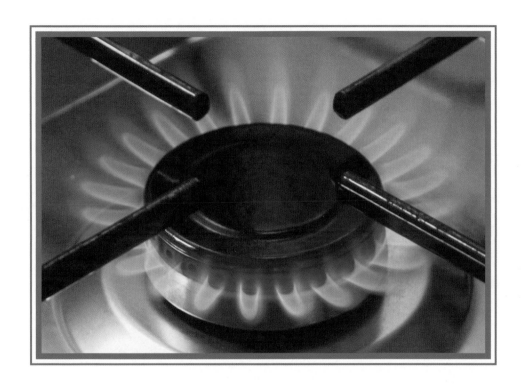

Extinguishing Fires

Fires are dangerous. Remember . . . stay back and call 911 so the firefighters can do their job.

Firefighters may use foam or water to **extinguish** fires.

How did you extinguish
your birthday candles?